LOST LINES OF WALES
RUABON TO BARMOUTH

TOM FERRIS

GRAFFEG

CONTENTS

FOREWORD

This series of books aims to revive nostalgic memories of some of the more interesting and scenic railways which served Wales and visitors to the country. It is still possible to travel by train over two sections of the route covered in this volume and many other miles of former railway track beds throughout Wales have been converted into footpaths, affording a more leisurely view of the often stunning countryside through which the trains once passed.

The subject of Welsh place names and their spelling is one which occupies many pages of print and can be a minefield for fluent speakers of the language let alone this nervous *dysgwyr*. Therefore, as this book is about railways, I have decided to adopt the spellings used by the railway operators. Where this changed over the years, so has the spelling in the book. Thus Dolgelley and Barmouth Junction become Dolgellau and Morfa

Mawddach from around 1960 and other quirks such as the name of Aberystwyth & Welch Coast Railway retains the solecism it had from the time of the Act of Parliament which brought it into existence.

Trains are often described as being either Up or Down services. For main lines terminating in London, trains heading to the capital are always Up services. In the case of the Ruabon to Barmouth Junction/Morfa Mawddach route, Down trains are heading for the coast and Up services are bound for Llangollen, Ruabon or Chester. Compiling this ramble back in time has given me enormous pleasure, *dw i'n gobeithio byddwch chi'n mwnhau y daith hefyd,* I hope you enjoy the journey too!

INTRODUCTION

The 1840s saw most of the construction of many of the lines which would form the core of the British railway network. In 1840, the Grand Junction Railway opened a line from Crewe to Chester, linking that border city to Birmingham and London. In 1844, two further railways serving Chester were authorised by Parliament. The Chester & Holyhead was promoted to drive a line across the north Wales coast to serve the port of Holyhead and become the route of the Irish Mails, while a more modest concern, the North Wales Mineral Railway, was launched to link Chester with the important industrial areas around Wrexham. In 1845, the NWM was given authority to extend its line five miles south from Wrexham to Ruabon but was then incorporated into a much bigger scheme in 1846, the Shrewsbury & Chester Railway which would connect those two places using the tracks of the NWM to reach Chester. The S&C line opened throughout in October 1848.

At that point, those Victorian promoters in north-east Wales paused for breath. Or, rather, the depressed national economic conditions which followed the collapse of the Railway Mania of the mid-1840s, caused them to pause in their efforts to expand the network in their area. It had been a period of intense speculation in railway stocks, which diminished in value when the bubble inevitably burst. However, they soon recovered their optimism and got back to planning new railways.

As confidence returned, the eyes of those promoters at first focused on Llangollen which, by the 1840s, had become a place of some importance. As early as 1847 proposals had been discussed for building a railway down the Dee Valley to that town and possibly beyond. When the S&C opened it built a station called Llangollen Road between Chirk and Ruabon from where coaches conveyed passengers to the town. Llangollen's origins date back to a church built in the sixth century and its importance as a crossing point on the River Dee was confirmed when a stone bridge was built over the river at the behest of the Bishop of St. Asaph in the fourteenth century. By the nineteenth century, the areas around Llangollen were producing coal, slate and lime and the town became a staging post on the Holyhead Road which was built in the 1830s by Thomas Telford on behalf of the government to expedite the Irish Mails on their journey from Dublin via Holyhead to London. The improved transport links provided by the Holyhead Road and the later railway began also to attract intrepid Victorian tourists to that most beautiful valley in which Llangollen is situated.

From 1805, Llangollen was also connected to the national canal system almost by accident. The Ellesmere Canal had originally been intended to link the Severn, the Dee and the Mersey but that part of its plan, for a navigation from Pontcysyllte to Chester, was abandoned, leaving Llangollen on the end of a long branch of what became the Shropshire Union canal system. On that branch are two of the finest engineering achievements of the canal age in Britain. The first of these is the

Chirk aqueduct, 70ft high and 710ft long, which carries the navigation across the Ceiriog Valley on the border between England and Wales. It has been eclipsed since the late 1840s by the parallel and adjacent viaduct carrying the Shrewsbury to Chester railway on a higher level, almost a metaphor in stone for how the railways supplanted the canals as the dominant form of inland transport in Britain in the nineteenth century. A few miles further on, the canal is taken over the valley of the River Dee on the breathtaking 1,007 ft long Pontcysyllte aqueduct. Built by Thomas Telford and William Jessop and opened in 1805, the canal is carried in a cast iron trough supported by nineteen masonry pillars 126ft high. The section of the Llangollen Canal from just beyond the English border to the Horseshoe Falls at Llangollen, including the aqueducts at Chirk and Pontcysyllte, was awarded the status of a World Heritage Site by UNESCO in 2009.

Railway promotion in the Dee Valley got under way again in the early 1850s. Several schemes were mooted. One was for a line to link Ruabon to Rhyl, on the C&H line, via Llangollen. Another proposed a branch from Cefn on the S&C line but the one which was approved by Parliament was the Vale of Llangollen Railway whose Act for a line from Ruabon to Llangollen received Royal Assent in August 1859. This scheme was backed by the Great Western Railway who worked the line which opened for goods traffic on 1st December 1861 and for passenger trains from 2nd June 1862. The GWR already had its eyes on the distant shores of Cardigan Bay and on the north Wales coast and, even as the navvies were building the Llangollen line, its promoters were planning to extend it. An Act authorising a line from Llangollen to Corwen was passed in August 1860 and this opened in May 1865. Corwen now became a junction for two railways as the town had been reached by the Denbigh, Ruthin & Corwen line coming in from the north the previous year. Some complex railway politics now ensued. The GWR had designs on taking over the DR&C and the Vale of Clwyd line, which linked it to the Chester to Holyhead line at

Rhyl, but these ambitions were thwarted when those lines became part of the empire of one of the GWR's great rivals, the London & North Western Railway.

In 1861 the Aberystwyth & Welch Coast Railway was authorised to build a line from Aberystwyth to Barmouth and Pwllheli. Further north, thoughts turned to extending the line from Llangollen to connect with the A&WCR. As often happened in the nineteenth century when an opportunity such as this appeared, a plethora of schemes were mooted. Those which Parliament approved were: an extension of the A&WCR from what would become Barmouth Junction to Dolgelley; an extension of the existing railway through the Dee Valley from Corwen to Bala; and a third scheme linking the other two, the Bala & Dolgelley Railway. The effect of these Acts passed in 1862 was to deprive the GWR of a through line to the coast and this seemed to have somewhat diminished the enthusiasm of those in control at Paddington for the project. Another seven years would pass before trains ran through from Ruabon to Barmouth Junction.

Construction on the line south from Corwen began and it opened as far as Llandrillo in 1866. Trains through to Bala began to operate from 1st April 1868. The 17¼ mile long Bala & Dolgelley line was also under construction and the inspector from the Board of Trade passed it as fit for traffic, services beginning on 4th August 1868. The navvies were also busy further west, building the line from Dolgelley to Barmouth Junction which the A&WCR had reached in July 1865. The year before, a new and significant name in Welsh railway history emerged when several of the smaller companies operating in mid Wales and Shropshire amalgamated to form the Cambrian Railways. The A&WCR became part of the CR in 1865 and what was now the CR's branch to Dolgelley opened as far as Penmaenpool in July 1865. Then, in 1866, the British economy was plunged into crisis when the major London bank Overend & Gurney failed with liabilities of about £11 million. This put a brake on railway promotion and much else and its ripples were felt in west Wales where the CR struggled to raise the funds to complete its line to Dolgelley. The GWR and the B&D obtained powers to build the line if the CR did not open it by August 1869. This seemed to concentrate the minds of the CR directors who managed to find the resources to do this, thwarting the GWR and its ally. The fact that two companies operated into Dolgelley led to the unusual situation of two stations on the one site. Each company controlled one side of the station and both had their own station masters! By 1896 the GWR, who had worked the whole line from the outset, had absorbed the nominally independent companies which had built the route from Ruabon to Dolgelley. Then, in 1923 the government sponsored the amalgamation of Britain's railway companies into four large groups. At the grouping, the CR became part of an enlarged GWR, allowing Paddington to at last achieve a long held ambition and control the whole line through to Barmouth Junction.

One other addition to the railway map of this part of Wales must be mentioned as it did impact upon our line. In the early 1870s, the GWR and the Dee Valley companies heavily backed the Bala & Festiniog Railway which was authorised to build a line to link those two places. At Festiniog the existing narrow gauge line from there to Blaenau would be converted to standard gauge and thus the GWR would reach one of the great centres of the Welsh slate industry. This had hitherto been the preserve of the Festiniog Railway whose narrow gauge line had been bringing slates down to Portmadoc on the coast for onward transit by sea since the 1830s. The FR's monopoly was challenged in 1878 when the L&NWR extended its branch up the Conwy Valley from Llandudno Junction to reach Blaenau Festiniog.

Lavishly engineered through some of the most remote country in Wales, the GWR backed line opened throughout in September 1883 but it failed to generate any significant amount of slate traffic and remained a most picturesque backwater throughout its existence. This line met the route from Llangollen at a new location called Bala Junction. The original Bala station on the line to Dolgelley was replaced by a new one on the branch close to the eastern fringes of the town. In 1934, the GWR opened Bala Lake Halt on the site of the original station. Much later this was to become the site of the terminus of the narrow gauge Bala Lake Railway and is thus today the only railway station left in Bala.

It had taken the best part of ten years to build the 54½ miles from Ruabon to Barmouth Junction. Much effort and treasure had gone into constructing what became no more than a secondary main line throughout its existence. Beyond Llangollen there was little in the way of industry, the line serving small rural communities. In the 1861 census Corwen and Dolgelley had populations of about 2,000 and Bala 1,300.

The pattern of train services did not vary greatly throughout the lifetime of the route. There were generally two or three through trains daily between Ruabon and Barmouth. The most intensive services ran in the inter-war period when there were up to six through trains. Some services were extended beyond Ruabon to Chester and even Birkenhead. The Dee Valley trains connected at Ruabon with services from Shrewsbury, Birmingham and London Paddington. In addition to the through services there were additional short workings between Llangollen and Ruabon. As many as six trains shuttled between these two locations daily. Other short workings ran over parts of the line such as from Bala to Dolgelley. In addition there was a shuttle service at the southern end of the line from Barmouth Junction to Dolgelley providing connections into services on the line from Dovey Junction to Pwllheli. There was also a service from Bala Junction to the station in the town connecting with trains on the main line. A variety of goods trains also served stations along the route throughout its existence.

The railway from Ruabon to Barmouth Junction was much busier in summer than in winter. The GWR did much to promote the seaside resorts it served along the shores of Cardigan Bay. To this day, the distinctive twang of a Birmingham or a Manchester accent is commonly heard on the beach at Barmouth on a fine summer afternoon and Llangollen, then as now, was also a popular destination for excursionists. The GWR opened a series of halts along the length of the line from the early twentieth century onwards to accommodate both locals and visitors and attract additional traffic to its trains. The railway also provided secure and regular employment throughout its length. For example, GWR staff returns show that in 1935 Llangollen station provided employment to 13, Corwen 22 and Dolgelley 19. In an area where employment opportunities were limited, the boost which country railways such as this gave the local economy should not be underestimated.

The beginning of the end of this, and many other secondary lines, was the development of road transport in the years following the Great War. Lorries, coaches and increasing numbers of private cars provided alternatives to the railway's effective monopoly of goods and passenger transport which had pertained up to 1914. Given the limited traffic potential of the area it served once road transport began to bite into that, the economic prospects for the route began to darken. The Second World War put a temporary halt to the unstoppable rise of the internal combustion engine but with increasing prosperity and car ownership in the 1950s, traffic inexorably declined. In the face of this increasing competition, there was no attempt to modernise the railway. It remained almost exclusively steam worked with locomotives latterly being supplied for the most part by Croes Newydd depot in Wrexham and a much smaller shed at Penmaenpool. Diesel locomotives and railcars were scarcely ever seen on any of its services. The line from Bala Junction to Blaenau Festiniog closed to passengers in January 1960 and to goods trains in January 1961, though a short length was retained from Blaenau to Trawsfynydd for traffic to the nuclear power station there. Then, in 1963, the infamous Beeching Report was published which sounded the death knell for thousands of miles of Britain's railways. The report earmarked for closure three of the four railways which served the coast of Mid Wales. The axe hung over both the Ruabon to Barmouth and Shrewsbury to Aberystwyth lines. If only as the lesser of two evils, the right one probably survived.

Confirmation that the line was to close came in 1964 and services ended on 2nd November of that year. However, because of the delay in organising replacement bus services, the line had a temporary stay of execution and train services actually resumed on 23rd November. This was short lived as nature intervened. Flooding at various points along the route had occurred from time to time since it opened.

Indeed the most serious incident in its whole history had been due to flooding. In September 1945, close to Sun Bank Halt between Trevor and Llangollen, the Shropshire Union Canal which was adjacent to the line burst its banks causing the railway trackbed to be washed away leaving a section of track suspended in mid air. The first train of the day carrying goods and mail was derailed and the engine driver was killed when the train plunged down the embankment. On the night of December 12th, flooding breached the line in two places, near Dolgellau and to the east of Bala. Passenger services continued to operate from Dolgellau to Bala and from Llangollen to Ruabon but, as a second closure date had, by then, already been fixed for 18th January 1965, no attempt was made to repair the flood damage and no through trains ran along its whole length again.

The line, like so many victims of Doctor Beeching's infamous axe was set to meekly exit from the pages of the history of Britain's railways. Or not quite, as it turned out. Freight services lingered on to serve a chemical plant near Trevor until January 1968 and between Ruabon and Llangollen until April of that year. Shortly afterwards work began to rip up the track along the route. Then, in the early 1970s, a scheme was promoted to rebuild the section of line from Bala to Morfa Mawddach. This proposal for a narrow gauge line close to 30 miles long was not proceeded with but a more realistic plan for a narrow gauge line along the shore of Llyn Tegid/Bala Lake took shape. A new company Rheilffordd Llyn Tegid Ltd (Bala Lake Railway Ltd) was formed, which is claimed to be the first business to be registered in the Welsh language. Trains began running on the 2ft gauge line in August 1972 from Llanuwchllyn station, which became the headquarters of the new railway. The line was opened as far as Bala Lake Halt in March 1976 giving a run of some 4½ miles, mostly along the shores of the lake. Llanuwchllyn station has been beautifully restored indeed, it has been enhanced with a canopy on the platform which it did not have in GWR or BR days. This was rescued from Aberdovey station. The signal box on the Up platform is used to handle traffic on the narrow gauge line. The steam locomotives used on the line were originally built to work in slate quarries in north Wales.

Other parts of the former railway have met differing fates. All traces of Dolgellau station and the track bed through the town were obliterated with the building of a bypass road in the 1970s. The section of track from Penmaenpool to Morfa Mawddach has been transformed into a delightful footpath which skirts the estuary and a visitor to Llangollen today might think for a moment that they had stepped out of a time machine. For decades, the cameras of many of those who came to Llangollen, standing on the bridge over the River Dee, had been trained onto the long curving platforms of the station below. Photographs taken after the line closed and the tracks had been lifted presented a sad perspective on this once bustling scene. The 1970s saw groups of railway enthusiasts throughout the country, reeling from

the effects of the Beeching Report and the end of steam traction in Britain in 1968, begin to plan to rebuild sections of closed and disused lines on which they could run steam locomotives. One such group in north Wales at first thought of reviving the branch line from Dyserth to Prestatyn but soon switched their attention to restoring the railway that once ran through Llangollen.

They began to restore the station in 1975 and, at first, progress was slow but by 1986 trains could run to the first station beyond Llangollen, at Berwyn. Since then the line has been extended in stages to Glyndyfrdwy (1993) and Carrog (1996) and, with assistance from the Welsh Government, the track has been relaid to a new station, Corwen East, services to the town resuming in October 2014. An incredible amount has been achieved since 1975. The Llangollen Railway has built a workshop on the site of the former goods yard and restored a number of steam locomotives for use on the line, including examples of former GWR steam locomotives types which ran on the

line in its heyday. The visitor to Llangollen can once again enjoy the sight and sound of steam-hauled trains snaking round the curved platforms through the station. They may no longer be able to take their passengers to the coast of Cardigan Bay but a journey on the line, which follows the River Dee closely as it curves through this most picturesque valley, perhaps in a train hauled by a green liveried Great Western locomotive, its brass-work sparkling in the sunshine, is a memorable and enjoyable experience. It is a joyful recreation of the railway which served this attractive and interesting part of Wales for close to one hundred years.

RUABON
JUNCTION FOR
LLANGOLLEN
CORWEN
BALA FESTINIOG
DOLGELLEY & BARMOUTH

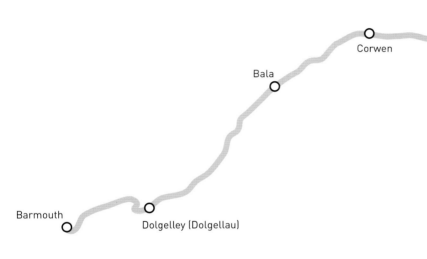

Barmouth
Dolgelley (Dolgellau)
Bala
Corwen
Ruabon

We will begin our journey to the coast at Ruabon which is still served today by trains running between Shrewsbury and Chester. It is however, a pale shadow of its former glory seen in this view from the summer of 1952 as former GWR Hall class 4-6-0 No 4991 *Cobham Hall* arrives at the station with train from Shrewsbury. An impressive range of destinations in Wales could then be reached by train from here.

Most trains for the Llangollen line started from the bay platform at Ruabon. On 17th April ex-GWR 2-6-0 No 7310 waits there at the head of the 3.00pm service from Wrexham to Pwllheli.

The line to the coast diverged just south of Ruabon station with the first section as far as Llangollen being double track. On 16th August 1952, ex-GWR 2-6-0 No 5310 joins the Birkenhead to Paddington main line at the junction with a goods train which was running from Pwllheli to Chester, under the watchful eyes of two permanent way men.

The first station on the line was at Acrefair. The name is believed to have originated from the Welsh for Mary's acre and related to a piece of land given to a monastery in honour of the Virgin. Belying its romantic medieval origins, this was a heavily industrialised area with chemical and brick manufactories providing traffic for the goods trains on the line. In this 1960s view, a short goods train is seen in the cutting just outside Acrefair station hauled by British Railways Standard class 4 4-6-0 No 75071.

The next station soon followed. Trevor was in the heart of the industrial belt. It had a short branch to a brick works which diverged to the right of the signal box at the top of the picture and a freight-only line from Pontcysyllte which trailed in through the goods yard on the left. This view was taken from the bridge which carried the Ruabon to Llangollen road over the railway.

The line continued through Sun Bank Halt, opened in 1905 and the scene of the fatal accident referred to in the Introduction, before reaching Llangollen some 5½ miles from the junction with the main line. The classic view of the station has always been that taken from the bridge over the River Dee. In this image dating from the Summer of 1953, an Autotrain for Ruabon is about to depart from the Up platform. This was a method of operation much favoured by the GWR on branch and secondary lines. For the journey to Ruabon, the tank locomotive manned by the fireman, will remain at the rear of the train and propel the specially designed carriages ahead of itself. The driver sits in the front coach where he has controls linked to those on the locomotive to regulate the speed of the train, apply its brakes and operate the warning gong above one of the front windows. This method of operating meant that the engine did not have to run round the carriages at the end of a journey, speeding up turn round times. This Autotrain is on one of the short workings from Ruabon to Llangollen which were a feature of the timetable for many years. The long curving platforms of the station continue well beyond the train and the covered footbridge spanning the tracks.

Looking in the other direction, a through train from Birkenhead to Barmouth arrives at Llangollen station on 19th May 1951, hauled by GWR 2-6-0 No 7305. This was a long lived GWR design of mixed traffic locomotives dating from 1911 which, as we will see, were regular performers on this line.

The next part of our journey from Llangollen to Corwen is one which can still be enjoyed today on one of the trains operated by the Llangollen Railway. Because the station was on a cramped site beside the river the town's goods facilities were located about ½ mile to the west. Access was controlled by Llangollen Goods Line Junction signal box and this marked the end of the double track section. The line then swings across the River Dee before passing through Berwyn station with its imposing mock Tudor station building. It then passes through the 689 yard long Berwyn Tunnel. There is a place where trains could cross at Deeside Loop before the next station, Glyndyfrdwy, is reached.

Our view of the station was taken on a sunny 8th May 1935 and shows GWR Dean Goods loco No 2555, a design dating from the 1880s, hauling an Engineer's Inspection Saloon stopped opposite the signal box on the Up platform where it remains today.

The line has been running close to the river all the way from Llangollen and the next station west of Glyndyfrdwy is Carrog, 13 miles from Ruabon. This has been the terminus of the steam railway for some years pending its extension to Corwen. It is rather busier these days and the sidings in the goods yard to the left are usually full of LR stock. This undated view shows the station in its original condition before it became the temporary terminus of a major visitor attraction.

CORWEN

Corwen is an attractive market town in the Dee Valley and, in its heyday, it was an important railway centre which had its own engine shed up to 1927. It was the junction where the line from Ruabon met the former L&NWR line that ran south from Rhyl through Denbigh. This view looking west in August 1949 shows the goods depot to the left of the picture. With the extension of the LR, the sound of steam locomotives at work can once again be heard in Corwen for the first time since the 1960s.

Less than two miles south-west of Corwen was the next station, Cynwyd. There was no passing loop or signal box here but it did have sidings, a goods shed and loading pens for livestock.

The line continued to run close to the river and the next station, Llandrillo, 2½ miles on from Cynwyd, was a more substantial affair. It had a passing loop and a signal box which was located on the Down platform. The sizeable goods shed can be seen beyond the signal box in this undated view.

For a not very populous and largely rural part of the country, the stations on this line were surprisingly close together. After another short run of about 2½ miles, in which the line crossed and recrossed the river on two stone bridges, trains reached Llandderfel. This was the railhead for a number of small villages in the vicinity. A train from Ruabon enters the station hauled by one of the ubiquitous ex-GWR 2-6-0s No 7310. The signal to the left of the locomotive for trains heading in the other direction is of interest. Called a banner repeater, it shows drivers of departing trains the aspect of the Up starting signal. This was beyond the road bridge and thus was rather obscured by it. With a train arriving off the single line section from Llandrillo both the repeater and the main signal are at danger.

BALA

With the railway still staying close to the River Dee, 3½ miles from Llandderfel, Bala Junction was soon reached. This was one of a number of locations both in Wales and throughout the British Isles which would not have existed without the coming of the railways. In this case Bala already had a station on the line to the coast, albeit some distance for the centre of the town, and it was the building of the line to Blaenau Festiniog which led to the construction in the early 1880s of Bala Junction and the new Bala Town station on the branch. Bala Junction had no road access, it was purely a place where people changed trains.

Located adjacent to the river some 27 miles from Ruabon, Bala Junction was a substantial station with three platforms. The branch diverged at the end of the island platform as can be seen in this view which shows GWR Pannier Tank No 7443 arriving at the junction from Bala Town.

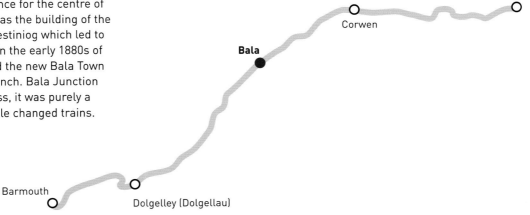

In this view of the station, taken on 2nd May 1963, there are no passengers, staff or trains to be seen. Country junctions such as this were often somnolent for long periods of time, interrupted by short bursts of frantic activity as trains arrived and departed and passengers, mail and parcels were transferred from one to the other. By this time the line beyond Bala to Blaenau Festioniog had been closed, though a connecting service ran between Bala Town and Bala Junction until the closure of the line to Ruabon in 1965.

Shortly after leaving Bala Junction, the line passed under a road bridge close to where the river joins Llyn Tegid (Bala Lake) and passed the site of the original Bala station which had opened in 1868. This closed when Bala Junction and Bala Town stations opened but was revived by the GWR as Bala Lake Halt in 1934. Its site is now the terminus of Rheilffordd Llyn Tegid/Bala Lake Railway and has been renamed Bala Penybont. Today narrow gauge trains follow the course of our line for 4½ miles as far as Llanuwchllyn. There were two halts on this section when it was a standard gauge line, Llangower and Glan Lynn. The current Llangower Halt on the narrow gauge line is to the west of the original GWR version and now boasts a passing loop. Glan Lynn has been replaced by a stop further west at Pentrepiod.

Llanuwchllyn was and remains an impressive station. It was rebuilt in its present form by the GWR in 1896. Most of its original features have been retained by its new owners, Rheilffordd Llyn Tegid/Bala Lake Railway, including the station building and the large GWR signal box on the Up platform.

As well as restoring the station to a high standard, it has been enhanced by the addition of a canopy in front of the main station building. This was something the GWR never got round to providing here.

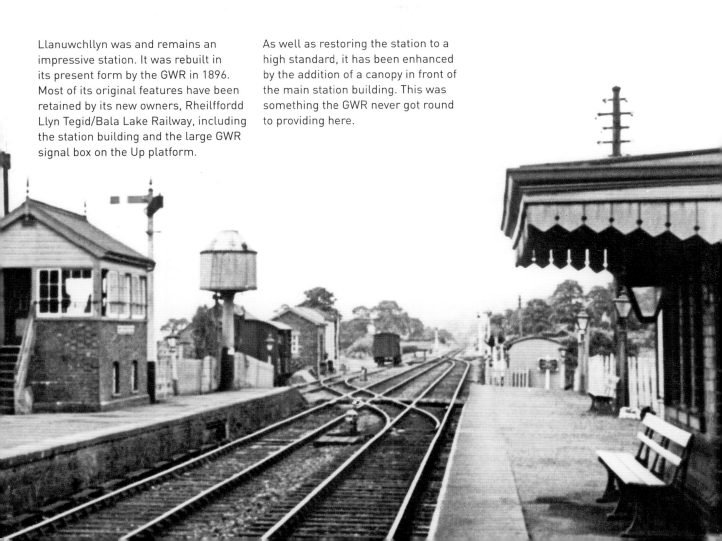

Trains cross at Llanuwchllyn on 2nd August 1963 hauled by locomotives from different eras. On the left is BR Standard class 4 4-6-0 No 75006 on a service to Barmouth whilst the Ruabon train is headed ex-GWR Manor class 4-6-0 No 7800 *Torquay Manor*. No 75006 is one of the 999 locomotives built by British Railways to its new Standard designs post-nationalisation in 1948. The GWR Manor class, of which No 7800 was the first built, dated from the late 1930s and were regular performers on this line. The Llangollen Railway has a preserved example of one of these engines, No 7822 *Foxcote Manor*, in its fleet.

The line had been relatively level most of the way from Ruabon but beyond Llanuwchllyn trains were met by some quite severe gradients. Leaving the station they faced a climb which was as steep as 1 in 63 in places. The summit was reached at Garneddwen where the GWR built a loop and a signal box in 1913 to provide a crossing point on the section from Llanuwchllyn to Drws Y Nant. A halt was provided here in the 1930s with staggered platforms, the only access being provided by a footpath from the Bala to Dolgelley road. On the way to Garneddwen, trains passed another halt opened in 1934 at Llys, whose modest facilities are seen here looking north.

From Garneddwen the gradients favoured coast-bound trains. On the 9 mile stretch from there to Dolgelley those running in the other direction faced a fairly continuous climb which ranged between 1 in 110 and 1 in 50 at its steepest as the line followed the Valley of the Wnion. The gradient for Up trains through Drws-y-Nant station was 1 in 64. In this 1950s view, ex-GWR 2-6-0 No 5315 is pulling hard to restart its train, the 2.35pm stopping service from Barmouth to Ruabon, from the station. The picture is undated but it was probably taken in the early spring as evidenced by the steam leaking from the heating pipes under the carriages. On what looks a fairly bleak day in mid Wales, at least the passengers on the train were being kept warm.

The steepest part of the climb up from Dolgelley with a gradient of 1 in 50 began just beyond the level crossing gates at Bontnewydd station, though this eased to 1 in 200 through the station. When the line was built there was no crossing place but the layout was remodelled in 1923 and a loop was added. A gradient as steep as 1 in 50 was very rare on Britain's railways. Coming down such a bank was as much a problem as going up, especially with a goods train which did not have continuous braking and had to be controlled by the skill of the driver at the front and the guard in his brake van at the rear. The traditional loose-coupled railway goods wagon from the age of steam only had a hand brake and, before descending an incline such as this, the train would stop to allow the guard to pin down the hand brakes on an appropriate number of wagons. If the crew misjudged the weight or went too fast, as happened occasionally on steeply graded lines, their train could easily run out of control.

This view was taken on 10th August 1963 from an elevated position on Bontnewydd bank. Working hard up the climb is a very special working, the Royal Train. This was taking the Queen and the Duke of Edinburgh on the long journey from an engagement in Aberdovey to Aberdeen for the traditional Royal summer vacation in Scotland. The train is hauled by a pair of ex-GWR Manor class 4-6-0s polished up to the nines for the occasion. The working of Royal Trains involved much railway special protocol including the running of a pilot locomotive ahead of the special to ensure the line was clear and a unique headcode of four oil lamps carried by the locomotive, three above the buffer beam and one on the smokebox. These can be seen on leading locomotive No 7819 *Hinton Manor*, another member of this class which is still with us, preserved on the Severn Valley Railway in Shropshire.

Ruabon

Corwen

Bala

Dolgelley (Dolgellau)

Barmouth

It is hard to believe today but Dolgelley was once an important station on this route. Until the 1923 railway grouping, there were effectively two stations here on the same site. This was a throwback to the time of the line's construction with the Cambrian Railway owning and operating the final section down to the coast at Barmouth Junction. Before then, at Dolgelley, the Down platform was Cambrian territory and the Up Great Western. There were two station masters and two signal boxes and the station buildings on the platforms were quite different in terms of their architectural style. On 9th August 1948

the 8.30am service for Barmouth is seen about to depart from the former Cambrian platform at the station. The locomotive, ex-GWR 0-4-2T No 1434, is sandwiched in the middle of its two Auto Trailers.

DOLGELLAU

By way of comparison, the GWR buildings on
the Up platform at Dolgellau are seen beyond
an unidentified British Railways Standard
Tank locomotive which has just arrived with
a service from Barmouth.

Like so many of the stations on this line, that at Dolgelley was close to a river, in this case the Afon Wnion. The river can be seen to the right of the 2-6-0 No 7310 arriving with a goods train bound for Barmouth in August 1948.

A busy moment at Dolgelley station on 9th August 1948. The starting signal has dropped for ex-GWR 2-6-0 No 4375, at the head of the 1.12pm Barmouth to Ruabon passenger train. Steam is blowing from her safety valves indicating that the fireman had generated the good head of steam necessary for the locomotive to negotiate the hilly road ahead of her. Dating from 1915, No 4375 was one of the oldest survivors of the class still in service at this time. Two unidentified sister locomotives are also in the picture.

In contrast to what had pertained east of Dolgelley, the final part of the line from Dolgelley to Barmouth Junction was devoid of any serious gradients. Returning to a familiar pattern, the railway followed a river which, from its meeting with the Afon Wnion, was the Afon Mawddach which gradually broadened out to form an estuary. This section is the third part of the line which continues to offer a form of public transport to this day. The trackbed from Dolgellau to Morfa Mawddach and across the bridge to Barmouth has been converted into a 9 mile long footpath and cycle route called the Llwybr Mawddach Trail. It still affords the same stunning views available to passengers on the railway until the 1960s but from a lower perspective than that seen from a railway carriage. The first station after Dolgelley was Penmaenpool and this view shows a train entering the station around 1918. At this time the Cambrian Railways was still in existence and operating this part of the line, GWR services ending at Dolgelley. Arriving bunker first at the head of a local passenger train from Dolgelley is CR 0-4-4T No 3 which was built in 1895.

The original station at Penmaenpool had only one platform on the estuary side of the line but a second one was added by the GWR. There was also a railway-owned wooden toll bridge across the estuary here which is still in use. Located a few hundred yards west of the station was a small wooden shed which could house two engines. This remained in use until the line closed and was classed as a sub shed of Croes Newydd Depot in Wrexham. This photo shows Penmaenpool station, as rebuilt by the GWR, recorded on the 30th March 1958 showing its close proximity to the water's edge. The signal box is still in existence. Another example of the GWR's passion for corrugated iron as a building material, this time a shed or a lamp hut of some sort, is in the foreground.

PENMAENPOOL

PENMAENPOOL SIGNAL BOX

TO BARMOUTH JUNC
&
PWLLHELI TRAINS

For 4½ miles beyond Penmaenpool, the railway line continued to follow closely the shore of the estuary until it reached the final station before its junction with the coast line. This was Arthog, whose single wooden platform was on the landward side. There was never a passing loop here, though a siding was provided. On 13th August 1935, GWR 0-4-2T No 4812 and trailer No 164 have just crossed Arthog bridge with a Dolgelley to Barmouth auto-train.

On 28th May 1962 a passenger train for Barmouth approaches the crossing at Arthog station, headed by Manor class 4-6-0 No 7811 *Dunley Manor*. Beyond the salt marshes and the estuary the mountains of Snowdonia tower in the background.

NOTICE
ALL PERSONS FOUND TRESPASSING
ON THIS RAILWAY WILL BE
PROSECUTED AS THE LAW DIRECTS.
RHYBUDD
OS CEIR UNRHYW BERSON YN
TRESPASO AR Y FFORDD HAIARN
HON FE'I DYGIR YN GYFREITHIOL
GYFARBWYDD, Y CYFRAITH
TRWY ORCHYMYN

BARMOUTH JUNCTION

Ruabon

Corwen

Bala

Dolgelley (Dolgellau)

Barmouth

Barmouth Junction was in a spectacular if remote location, another one of those places which would not have existed without the coming of the railways. In stark contrast to the single platform request stop which is Morfa Mawddach today, in its prime it was a large station with five platforms which at one time boasted a refreshment room. The layout was in the form of a triangle with the station at the apex pointing across the estuary towards Barmouth. There were platforms to serve Up and Down trains on both the Ruabon line and that which ran along the coast and a terminal bay platform accessible directly only by trains on the inland route. There were no platforms on the third side of the triangle which had allowed through running from the direction of Dolgelley towards Tywyn and beyond. Latterley this part of the triangle was used mainly to turn steam locomotives. This undated view is looking towards the station from the direction of Barmouth. The lines to the left lead to Ruabon, those to the right to Dovey Junction.

This photograph was taken from the Up Ruabon platform at Barmouth Junction. Both trains are working on coast line services. BR Standard class 2MT 2-6-2T No 82020 is on a goods train which will be proceeding across Barmouth Bridge as soon as the passenger train hauled by ex-GWR Manor class 4-6-0 No 7808 *Cookham Manor* has arrived at the station. This is another member of this class which is still with us. It was preserved by the Great Western Society following its withdrawal by British Railways and is usually to be found at that great citadel of all things GWR which is the Society's Didcot Railway Centre in Oxfordshire.

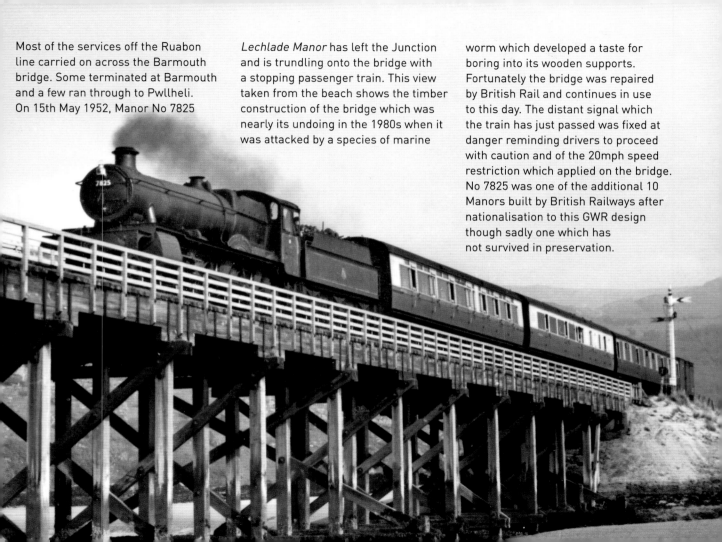

Most of the services off the Ruabon line carried on across the Barmouth bridge. Some terminated at Barmouth and a few ran through to Pwllheli. On 15th May 1952, Manor No 7825 *Lechlade Manor* has left the Junction and is trundling onto the bridge with a stopping passenger train. This view taken from the beach shows the timber construction of the bridge which was nearly its undoing in the 1980s when it was attacked by a species of marine worm which developed a taste for boring into its wooden supports. Fortunately the bridge was repaired by British Rail and continues in use to this day. The distant signal which the train has just passed was fixed at danger reminding drivers to proceed with caution and of the 20mph speed restriction which applied on the bridge. No 7825 was one of the additional 10 Manors built by British Railways after nationalisation to this GWR design though sadly one which has not survived in preservation.

CREDITS

Lost Lines of Wales – Ruabon to Barmouth published by Graffeg March 2016 © Copyright Graffeg 2016
ISBN 9781909823174
Author Tom Ferris

Graffeg Limited, 24 Stradey Park Business Centre, Mwrwg Road, Llangennech, Llanelli, Carmarthenshire SA14 8YP Wales UK
Tel 01554 824000 www.graffeg.com

Graffeg are hereby identified as the authors of this work in accordance with section 77 of the Copyrights, Designs and Patents Act 1988.

A CIP Catalogue record for this book is available from the British Library.

Photo credits

© Kidderminster Railway Museum: cover image and pages 13, 14, 18, 19, 20, 24, 27, 28, 31, 32, 33, 34, 37, 41, 42, 43, 44, 46, 47, 55, 56, 57, 59, 60, 62, 63.
© R. F. Roberts/SLS Collection: pages 17, 38, 65.
© P. Ward/SLS Collection: pages 23.
© W. A. Camwell/SLS Collection: pages 48, 50, 51, 52.

Other titles in this series:

Lost Lines of Wales
Cambrian Coast Line
ISBN 9781909823204

Lost Lines of Wales
Aberystwyth to Carmarthen
ISBN 9781909823198

Lost Lines of Wales
Brecon to Newport
ISBN 9781909823181